last ferry to skye

compiled by

Christopher J. Uncles

To the people of the island.

A woman in a white shawl and a tinker's caravan are waiting to 'cross the sea to Skye' in this turn of the century picture taken at Kyle of Lochalsh.

Richard Stenlake Publishing
1995

ISBN 1 872074 60 X

Published by
Richard Stenlake Publishing

Printed by
Cordfall Ltd, Glasgow
0141-332 4640

ACKNOWLEDGEMENTS

My grateful thanks are due to those who helped with my queries and/or allowed reproduction of photographs: Mrs Effie Campbell, Mrs Fiona Campbell, Robert Grieves, Ben Ireland (Miller Civil Engineering), Mrs Margaret Macdonald (Archivist, Clan Donald Lands Trust), Sir Iain Noble, John J. Patience, Vivienne Roberts (Isle of Skye Tourist Board), Sabhal Mor Ostaig, Colin M. Shields (Highland Communities NHS Trust), Talisker Distillery (United Distillers Plc), Alastair J.B. White. I am indebted to Lord Macdonald who kindly provided access to his family archives, and permitted reproduction of some previously unpublished photographs. Finally, my thanks are due in no small measure to my wife, Angela, for all her practical help, encouragement and patience throughout the preparation of the script.

Eribh suas, mata gu dileas,	Rise up, therefore, faithfully
Dhion bhur dùthcha 's cliù bhur sinnsear,	And protect your country and
Is bithibh seasmhach, fearail cruaidh,	The honour of your ancestry and be
An taic a chéile mar bu dual.	Steadfast, manly, hardy, together, as
Is cuimhnichibh air tìr nam beann	Was the custom and remember the land of
'S air gniomharan nan laoch a bh' ann,	Mountains, and the deeds of the bygone heroes
'S ged bhiodh bhur saothair searbh is buan,	And although your labours are intolerable
Cha robh na Gàidheil riamh gun bhuiaidh.	And unremitting – the Gaels were always winners.

(Taken from a postcard entitled 'Cuchullin Hills, Skye,' produced by the studios of George Washington Wilson).

To visit Skye is to make a progress into the 'dark backward and abysm of time'. You turn your back on the present and walk into antiquity. You see everything in the light of Ossian, as in the light of a mournful sunset.

A Summer in Skye, Alexander Smith, 1865.

INTRODUCTION

Those who know it are generally agreed that of all the islands which comprise the Inner Hebrides, Skye is something apart, something special. A large, tattered land mass stretching for some fifty miles, deeply indented by long sea lochs, no part of Skye is more than five miles from the sea. The Cuillins, the finest group of mountains in Britain, dominate the scene, catching the eye from every direction. Skye is a land where folklore, legend and fact are inextricably interwoven. Over the years it has been a destination for geologists, mountaineers and rock climbers, the haunt of artists, photographers, travellers and tourists. Many have felt compelled to record their experiences, and major and minor classics abound, with every imaginable aspect of island life having received the treatment.

The past is always close; memories are long and mental scars run deep. The Clearances, to make way for sheep, and the forced emigration of the eighteenth and nineteenth centuries, when whole communities were forcibly ejected to the New World and the Antipodes, are remembered vividly and with anguish. On occasions descendants of those involved have recounted to me these events of 150 years ago, speaking of them with such clarity that they could have taken place only last week. Such happenings shape present day attitudes and seem to permeate the very landscape even now.

Two great rival clans, the MacLeods and the MacDonalds, have fought over Skye. Prince Charles Edward Stuart fled briefly across the island in 1746 with a price of £30,000 on his head, but was never betrayed. Twenty seven years later those intrepid travellers, Samuel Johnson and James Boswell were to write about it in their journals and diaries. Sir Walter Scott immortalised the landscape in 1814 and J.M.W. Turner painted it. In Victorian and Edwardian times, Professor Norman Collie and his pioneering fellow climbers conquered those dramatic Cuillin peaks which rise to a height of over three thousand feet, straight from sea level. The assertion of a certain independence of spirit against landlord injustice (what we might nowadays call 'the troubles') led directly to the enactment of the Crofters' Holdings Act of 1886, a milestone in land law reform. Historical associations such as these mark this land out as unique.

Many recognise that the island has 'atmosphere', and the word intoxication has sometimes been used to describe the hold it has on tourists, many of whom return year after year. For my own part I felt the urge to make a first visit nearly thirty years ago, spurred on by the writings of Seton Gordon, Otta Swire and Alasdair Alpin MacGregor. My wife and I have returned again and again.

As I write, momentous developments are afoot on Skye. A toll bridge estimated to cost £25 million is in an advanced state of construction across the narrows from Kyle of Lochalsh, over Kyleakin Lighthouse Island and on to Skye at a point immediately adjacent to Kyle House at Kyleakin. To say that the project has not been without controversy would be an understatement. There is currently much concern in the communities which will be bypassed by the bridge, and if the experience here is the same as that suffered in the Highlands on completion of similar schemes, then those concerns are likely to be well justified. Travellers hurrying by will no longer stop and stare – or spend their money! An enhanced ferry service would have satisfied the needs of many, but the contract provides for this to be withdrawn when the bridge opens for business – the day when Skye technically ceases to be an island. For many who relished the short sea crossing, the experience of going 'Over the Sea to Skye' will have been irrevocably diminished. Whether for or against, most people would be forced to agree that one of the finest and purest views on earth will have been irretrievably impaired by this massive intrusion. For Skye this will provide a new beginning, and a judgement on the balance sheet of advantages and drawbacks can only be made in time. As an historical footnote, here are some statistics for Caledonian MacBrayne's busiest ferry route. In the last calendar year (1994) before the bridge opened, the Kyle to Kyleakin ferry carried 436,744 cars, 8790 coaches and commercial vehicles, and 1, 475,938 passengers.

It is at this crossroads in the island's history and development that I have compiled this collection of pictures of Skye, many of which are reproduced from postcards which were once commercially available. In general, little is known about the many publishers of these cards, and even less about the all important photographers who stood behind the camera and 'clicked' the shutter. However, the scenes that they recorded represent a valuable portrayal of the island's social history over the last century or so.

This selection is in no sense a present day guide to the island, as so much has altered since the pictures were taken. No doubt the coming of the bridge will bring more changes. I have attempted to make the choice of material as fully representative of the island as possible, and the picture sequence follows a route shaped broadly like a capital letter 'S'. Commencing at Portree, we will proceed through North Skye, return through the Cuillins, and finish in Sleat.

Whatever your interests, I hope that you find the selection interesting and above all, enjoyable.

Christopher J. Uncles.

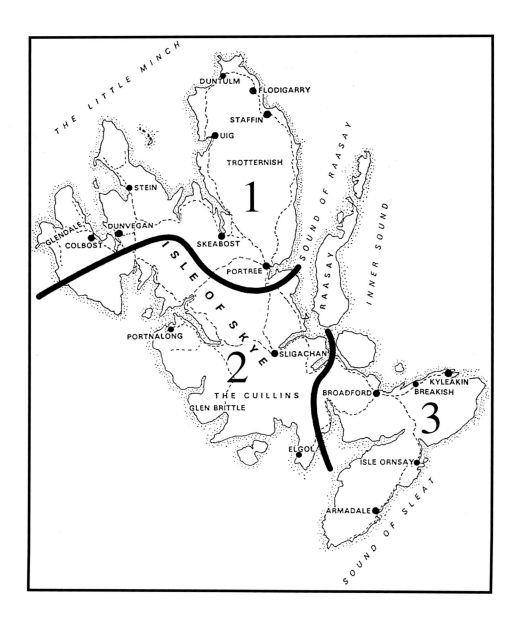

PORTREE TO GLENDALE

A hundred years ago the Post Office gave permission for little cards such as this to be issued. Known as Court Cards, they were the immediate forerunner of the picture postcard so familiar today. The whole of the back was given over to the address, leaving a small space for the message on the front. This example was produced especially for the Portree tourist trade, and the surrounding miniature line drawings depict some of the most popular attractions beloved by Victorian travellers. In 1900, when this card was posted, the population of Skye was 15,000 inhabitants.

The scene shown by this early 1930s photograph of Portree from Scorribreac is so very compact; a perfect anchorage surrounded by hills. Beaumont Crescent is overlooked by the Royal Hotel in the centre while, slightly to the right and behind lies the school, demolished forty years later. Portree's oldest building, the former town gaol, can be seen just behind the line of waterfront houses forming Quay Street. To the left on The Lump is the octagonal folly, since collapsed. In the distance, on the extreme left among the trees, is Viewfield House, formerly a family residence and now an hotel.

The Royal Hotel, which replaced the older MacNab's Inn, is renowned for being the place where Prince Charles Edward Stuart bade farewell to Flora MacDonald en route to Raasay, and later where Johnson and Boswell dined in 1773. A visitor to the hotel (now much enlarged) in the 1920s wrote with enthusiasm: 'Considerably cooler, but have been out the whole day with nothing but a cotton frock (at least, a few oddments *under* it) – all coats, gay jumpers and woollies of all kinds have *disappeared* this week! – most unusual on Skye! More than one told me *cotton's never* worn! All the folk seem to have them though. I've been on the 'bus' to the south end of island – the 'garden' district – more fertile and wooded – and a lovely shell beach – warm rock-pools, crabs, sea-urchins etc. etc.... It is still sultry – but the air on the hills is delightful – no sign of thunder – I'm learning to read the 'barograph' a new meteorological instrument they have here for foretelling weather – the barometer is going back to 'change', so expect heat wave passing. The hotel's very pleasant – v free and easy – not so many varieties and kickshaws on the menu as some places, but considering how remote we have plenty 'choices' and nice things to eat.'

In contrast to the opulence of the Royal Hotel is this picture of a crofter's cottage. This is a better than usual example of its type. Note the 'proper' chimney (often a barrel was pressed into service), additional netting to secure the thatch, and the absolutely essential peat stack.

A view along Bank Street, Portree, looking North. In the foreground, a group of barefoot children stand outside the Royal Hotel, while beyond, a horse and cart has just made the steep incline from the pier. The General Stores, known locally as the hardware store, can be seen between the trees. They belonged to Mr. J.G. Mackay, a man of strong convictions remembered for his fiery oratory. His business also advertised 'Yacht Stores', which no doubt provided a useful source of additional income from the many steam yachts and other vessels that used the harbour, especially during the season.

Quay Brae with a horse and cart passing the General Stores, this time in the opposite direction. The constant comings and goings at the pier provided plenty of business for local carriers. The former town gaol, the oldest extant building in Portree (circa 1810) and now the Tourist Information office, is visible through the trees in the centre of the picture. Both these views, taken in 1902, were sold through Mr. Mackay's store. The Rosedale Hotel now stands on this site.

Beaumont Crescent from the Meall with Bosville Terrace behind and to the right. In the foreground are several boats drawn up on the foreshore, some small neat garden plots, and poles for drying the fishing nets. The card is postmarked Portree, 25th July 1905 and carries a simple message: 'We arrived here from Tobermory; off to Dunvegan today'. It is addressed to the Laundry Maid at Barcaple, Ringford.

Herring fishing at Portree. At the time when this photograph was taken in 1902, herring fishing constituted one of the most important commercial activities in Scotland. Upwards of 7,000 boats were engaged in the Scottish fishing industry. They carried an aggregate of 230,000,000 square yards of netting, and the cured herring from their catches was worth one million pounds a year. The herring were migratory, with regular fishing in the Hebrides taking place in May and June. Large fleets of boats were required to satisfy the enormous demand for salt herring from Russia and Germany, and times were prosperous until the outbreak of the First World War in 1914. The few 'Zulu' herring boats tied up at the slipway (designed by Thomas Telford) give a quite false impression of the scale of activity carried on here, because during the season the harbour was often packed with fishing smacks.

Purchased by MacBrayne's in 1891, P.S. *Gael* was a familiar sight at most locations between Oban and Gairloch. With roads generally poor where they existed at all, sea lanes provided the natural means of communication, and Skye was well served by the MacBrayne fleet. Here the *Gael* is docking watched by a large number of people at the pierhead.

Another of the island's lifelines, MacBrayne's S.S. *Claymore*. In 1885 a week's tour from Glasgow to Stornoway could be taken calling at Oban, Tobermory, Portree and intermediate places: the cabin fare including 'superior accommodation' was 45/- (£2.25) or 80/- (£4), including meals.

70. S.S. "Glencoe" at Kyle.

Kyle Pharmacy Series.

Another familiar sight and much loved visitor to Portree and other Skye locations was the paddle steamer *Glencoe*. A veteran of the MacBrayne fleet, she served the west coast of Scotland for a record breaking 85 years, until 1931. Seen here arriving at Kyle with cattle on the bow deck, and probably other mixed cargo, including mail and passengers, the scene is captured by the camera of Duncan MacPherson of the Kyle Pharmacy. A conspicuous notice in one of the cabins read 'FOR 90 STEERAGE PASSENGERS WHEN NOT OCCUPIED BY CATTLE, ANIMALS, CARGO OR OTHER ENCUMBRANCES.' The card is postmarked 26th September 1912 and the message reads 'This steamer took us across to Skye. Pony and all'.

Bayfield, Portree. This card bears the retailer's name, J.A. Mackay, Watchmaker, etc., Portree and is likely to have been produced locally.

This photograph from the late 1920s, showing the garage and a little parade of shops (including Highland Home Industries) aptly serves to illustrate the changing face of Portree. The site, at the junction of Bank Street, Stormyhill Road and Bosville Terrace, is currently occupied by the Presto Supermarket.

The traditional Skye Cattle Markets or Trysts were held at Broadford, Sligachan, Fairy Bridge and Portree, the latter being established about 1580. This market stance is at Sluggans, north west of Portree, and was photographed about the turn of the century. By 1890 markets were being held here in May, August, September and November. Drovers, travellers and tinkers intermingled not only to discuss stock prices and transact the business, but also to exchange news and gossip. By all accounts, these were great family and social occasions! Writing in 1865, Alexander Smith's description of the Broadford fair is a classic: 'On either side of the road stood hordes of cattle, the wildest looking creatures with fells of hair hanging over their eyes, and tossing horns of preposterous dimensions. On knolls, a little apart, women with white caps and wrapped in scarlet tartan plaids, sat beside a staked cow or pony, or perhaps a dozen sheep, patiently waiting the advances of customers. Troops of horses neighed from stakes. Sheep were there, too, in restless throngs and masses, continually changing their shapes, scattering hither and thither like quicksilver, insane dogs and men flying along their edges. What a hubbub of sound!'

Portree from the North West, circa 1905, looking towards the bay. The school, in the middle foreground, was opened in 1875, demolished in the early 1970s and replaced by a building of little merit and alien to the immediate surroundings. Its present condition has recently been the subject of considerable concern and adverse comment in the local press and elsewhere. To the right is The Meall and Bayfield.

Braadford 21 Oct. 906
Sincieres salutations Cpretre

The boatman leans on his boat watching a man and two women work on the shore at Scorribreac, an arm of Portree Bay. Using the corran, a small hand sickle, they are cutting seaware (seaweed) which will be loaded into the wicker basket, before being taken back to the croft to be worked into the soil as a fertiliser. A common sight when this photograph was taken in the closing years of the 19th century.

Scorribreac Lodge, or more simply The Lodge, Portree. Lady Macdonald and her daughter, the Honorable Iona, spent the winter months here in the years either side of 1900. The family seat at Armadale Castle in Sleat was becoming a major financial burden, and the water penetration and resultant dampness that was ultimately to seal its fate years later was in evidence even at this time. Remembered as generous and kind-hearted, Lady Macdonald involved herself in good causes for the benefit of others in most of the town's local activities of the day. The Lodge is now the Cuillin Hills Hotel.

The Lodge Portree.

Writing in French to Madame Tailfer in Loiret, France in September 1910, Annie Murray described the lodge as follows: 'We are here with my cousins – a Scottish house especially built for hunting and the fishing of salmon and trout. From these windows there is a wonderful view of the sea and we are surrounded by mountains, lochs and rivers. Jessie and Flora have caught lots of fish to their great delight. We go out in the car and the motor boat belonging to my cousin.'

'Apart from the beautiful Episcopal church of St. Columba, with its gorgeous window dedicated to the memory of Skye's heroine, Flora MacDonald, the town itself has few architectural beauties.' So wrote Rev. J.A. MacCulloch, the then rector of this church when his best seller *The Misty Isle of Skye* was published in 1905. Today, the Tourist Board would probably not wish to dwell unduly on this aspect of the island's weather! The picture is of pre-First World War vintage.

ST COLUMBAS CHURCH & RECTORY, PORTREE.

Somerled Square looking into Wentworth Street. Despite the seeming inactivity of this scene, an observer once noted that 'the place swarms with shops!' The Macdonalds of the Isles trace their ancestry back to Somerled, the twelfth century Chief from which the Square takes its name, while other Macdonald family names are perpetuated in the town at Wentworth Street and Bosville Terrace.

Many Skye folk will recall this bus, which once operated under the company name of 'Skye Transport' of Wentworth Street. Around 1954 David MacBrayne acquired the Skye Transport operations, which were previously owned by the Scottish Cooperative Wholesale Society. SCWS also ran an Aberfeldy to Pitlochry service in Perthshire, and this photo was taken in Aberfeldy shortly after the bus was transferred from Skye, but before it was repainted with its new livery.

Postcards showing 'characters' either at work or play always sold well to the tourist trade, and sometimes the same pictures appeared in several locations, carrying quite different captions, and inferring that they were particular to that area. This card, entitled 'Octogenarian Spinner, Skye', and postmarked from Portree in August 1905 is written in Gaelic. The message reads 'Old woman carding wool for stockings in Portree. I know the house well.'

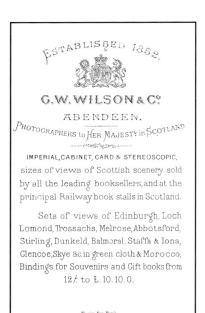

Crofters at Fisherfield, Portree. c1880.
This photograph came from the studio of George Washington Wilson, Photographers to Her Majesty in Scotland. The advert is taken from the reverse of one of his prints.

The despair in this picture, captioned 'Skye Crofters', is almost palpable. The life of crofters was a whole world away from that of 'the quality', with their large houses, shooting lodges and steam yachts moored in the bay. This picture is likely to have been taken in the last few years of the 19th century.

THE OLD MAN OF STORR, "AT HOME".

E.1608.

Noticing the strange rock formation on the skyline, a young woman travelling towards Portree asked what The Old Man of Storr was. His eyes twinkling mischievously, the man recounting the story at the bar replied: 'It is a phallic symbol associated with ancient fertility rites.' A stunned silence followed. A true exchange and another gentle leg-pull on a tourist by a Skye resident! In reality, this famous landmark is a wonderful rock obelisk about 160 feet high and 40 feet in diameter, which seems to be dangerously overhanging at the base when viewed at close quarters.

A neat croft in Staffin. Framed in their doorway, the family watch the photographer at work.

A number of districts in Skye seem to have their own quite separate identity and Staffin is one such place, with the Trotternish ridge and the ramparts of the Quiraing providing a dramatic backdrop to a most picturesque curved bay. In the centre of the picture, the poorly surfaced road running through the township glistens after a downpour.

Staffin Lodge. In the 1880s, parts of the island were in revolt when a few avaricious landlords increased rents arbitrarily, denying crofters adequate land to provide a living. During 1884, armed marines were despatched to Skye to quell the unrest on Major Fraser's Kilmuir Estates. Landed from warships at Uig, the men were marched overland through the Quiraing and Brogaig to Staffin, where some were billeted at the Lodge. This display of force was met with astonishment and jeering by crofters. A Sheriff-Officer was pelted with clods, stones and 'filth of all kinds' while trying to serve legal papers, and the crofters refused to either pay the increased rents, or appear in Court. The evictions were eventually abandoned, and the residents' grievances ultimately addressed by The Crofters' Act of 1886, a milestone in land law reform.

This photograph of Brogaig, Staffin shows the more usual method of travel before the coming of the motor car. The house at the corner of the road, behind the bridge, is Burnbank.

The fast flowing Kilmartin River, the church in the background, and the orderly hay stooks in front of the Post Office all combine to give this picture a sense of rural tranquillity.

The small hamlet of Digg, situated in the shadow of the Quiraing, photographed c1940. Note the mixture of old and newer housing.

THE ROAD OVER THE QUIRAING, SKYE.

The Quiraing is composed of basalt, and landslips and centuries of weathering have resulted in fantastic rock formations, shattered pinnacles and detached bastions. The best known features are The Needle, The Prison and The Table. If you have a good imagination, the gradually emerging mute shapes can be quite unsettling when alone in the Quiraing on a misty day. Even by mid-Victorian times over fifty people a day would travel out from Portree to scramble over the hillsides and take in the magnificent vistas. This 1931 view shows the road between Staffin and Uig as it crosses Trotternish at the Quiraing.

The superbly situated Flodigarry House was built as a private residence in 1895 by Major R.L. MacDonald, and became an hotel in 1928. He was a descendant of the legendary Flora MacDonald who had assisted the escape of Bonnie Prince Charlie after his defeat at Culloden in 1746. Five years after these historic events she married Allan MacDonald of Kingsburgh, settling in a cottage close by the hotel and farming the land hereabouts for several years.

FLODIGARRY HOTEL, ISLE OF SKYE

A little fishing instruction on the Staffin River, c1930. This card, entitled 'How to land a salmon', is one of a series bearing the overprint 'Flodigarry House Hotel, Skye' on the reverse.

This photograph of the castle and settlement at Duntulm is taken from an unusual perspective. It is said that after sunset and in the gathering gloom of twilight, ghostly armies of kilted warriors have been seen parading, fully armed, in readiness for battle on the ground between the Lodge (now an hotel), and the castle in the left of the picture. Indeed, from time to time, a body of Highlanders has been seen to pass right through the Lodge as though it did not exist......

The Ruins of Duntulm Castle, Isle of Skye.
An Ancient Stronghold of the MacDonalds of the Isles.

HAND SPINNING IN SKYE

PHOTO BY
SETON GORDON

Duntulm Castle occupies an impressive position on a high promontory and is impregnable on three sides, protected by sheer cliffs and the sea. Kilmuir, dubbed 'the granary of Skye' on account of its rich soil, was much coveted and fought over by the MacLeods and the Macdonalds of the Isles. The castle became the Macdonald's stronghold until about 1730. Pillaged over the years for building materials, and ravaged by the elements, it is a shadow of its former self, as year by year a little more of the structure collapses.

Synonymous with the district of Kilmuir is the name of the late Seton Gordon CBE, FZS (1886-1977), who lived at Upper Duntulm for many years. A well known author, photographer and player of the pibroch, he was also much respected for his great knowledge of the natural life of the region. 'Hand Spinning in Skye' is one of his photographs. Note the spinner's traditional shawl and the somewhat unusual elaborate carving on the spinning wheel itself.

Both the pictures on this page are from the camera of Seton Gordon. 'Sheep Shearing in Skye' shows a busy scene in the shadow of the Trotternish ridge in Kilmuir. At least twenty people are at work, and the ground is flecked with pieces of white fleece. The traditional date for shearing in Skye was mid-June. In the days before the advent of mechanical or electrical shears, the task was carried out by hand, and was hard work. However, it is another example of a communal activity which also doubled as a social occasion. Sometimes, groups of travelling shearers toured the townships offering their services and became familiar visitors year after year.

This is also a Kilmuir scene. The 'cas chrom' or foot-plough has now been consigned to folk museums, but was once in common usage. Note the neat crofts and, near the wheelbarrow, a pile of seaweed which will be worked into the soil. A few chicken – quite definitely free range – complete the scene!

A pony and trap and a smartly turned-out young lad are photographed in front of the Manse at Kilmuir. The track leads to Flora MacDonald's monument, which is just visible in the extreme left of the picture. The card is postmarked Uig, 3rd November 1919.

In the small burying ground at Kilmuir, the grave of Flora MacDonald is marked by a granite Celtic cross overlooking the sea. She had played a decisive part in the turbulent events of the '45, assisting the escape of Prince Charles Edward Stuart after the battle of Culloden. Buried here in 1790, it was said that her funeral was the largest ever known in Skye. The cortege was immense – more than a mile in length – and consisting of several thousands of people of every rank, both from Skye and the adjacent Isles. The procession was estimated to have consumed no fewer than three hundred gallons of whisky on its sixteen mile trudge to the graveyard with her coffin.

MONKSTADT HOUSE, KILMUIR, SKYE.

Having survived a perilous crossing of the Minch in an open boat, the fugitive Prince Charles Edward Stuart, accompanied by Flora MacDonald and several crew, landed on the Kilbride shore about a mile from Monkstadt House late in June 1746. This was the residence of Sir Alexander and Lady Margaret MacDonald. The Prince, disguised as a maid-servant, succeeded in evading his captors with the help of Flora, and subsequently followed an escape route that took him to Kingsburgh, Portree, Raasay, Elgol and into exile abroad. Sadly, Monkstadt House was unroofed in 1956 – to avoid payment of rates, it is said – and is now a forlorn crumbling shell.

The pier at Uig was extended in 1894 at a cost of £9,000, and this rather charming photograph was taken a few years later. These days Uig pier provides a car ferry link with Lochmaddy and Tarbert in the Outer Isles, courtesy of Caledonian MacBrayne.

Uig Bay, Loch Snizort, from North-West

Situated in a hilly amphitheatre with basalt cliffs at either side, Uig is grouped around another of the island's beautiful bays. Sparsely populated, and with the same wooded glens, cultivated strips and well maintained crofts, surprisingly little has changed in these two photographs taken sixty five years apart. Certainly the houses are much improved – a process given impetus, no doubt, by the Crofters' Holdings Act of 1886 which provided security of tenure and made provision for the fixing of fair rents.

UIG AND LOCH SNIZORT, SKYE.   B.5210.

Uig Village, Isle of Skye

When Major William Fraser acquired the Kilmuir and Uig Estates from Lord Macdonald, he immediately implemented changes to enhance his income. Some crofters were evicted and resettled elsewhere at considerably higher rents, while others who stayed put suffered crippling rent increases. As a result, the area became a focus for considerable crofter-resentment. In October 1877 after a long spell of atrocious weather, the river Conon, swollen to an immense torrent, burst its banks and as it rushed towards the bay swept away the ancient village burial ground and destroyed Uig Lodge, the Major's residence. Locals thought it an act of divine intervention.

Skeabost House is situated on the River Snizort at the head of the Loch of the same name. It was completed in 1871, having been enlarged from a sporting lodge built by the MacDonalds twenty years earlier. Nowadays, it combines all the comforts of a first class hotel with the best of the past, as seen in the original Scots pine panelling in the dining room and the Billiards room, complete with its Edwardian rules. The River Snizort is the longest river in Skye and much loved by anglers.

6930. Farewell to the Old Homestead, Isle of Skye.

Highland Cattle on Trek, Isle of Skye. 6931.

This pair of sequentially numbered 1920s photographs, published by J.B. White of Dundee, show cattle on the move on what is now the old road to Skeabost, near the former school at Bernisdale. The titles of the cards are strongly reminiscent of the old droving days, when cattle shipped from the Outer Isles joined others on Skye, streaming through Bracadale, Sligachan and Braes, down Glen Arroch and across the narrows to Glenelg, heading for the markets of Falkirk and Crieff. In this case they are more likely destined for the cattle market at Portree, or perhaps being driven to Kyleakin for shipment to Kyle in an open boat prior to their conveyance to the markets further south.

The Church and Manse at Snizort form the background for this 1922 pastoral scene. Once, this small settlement at the junction of the Portree to Uig and Dunvegan roads was noted for the mile of beech hedges along the Skeabost House boundary. But it has greater claims to fame, and the ever warring MacLeods and MacDonalds fought a bloody battle here in 1539. Mary MacPherson, a Skye poetess who wrote a number of poems about the evictions, was born here in 1821, and an ancient burying ground on St. Columba's Isle in the river is associated with the Saint who brought Christianity to the North.

Taken at Bernisdale, this photograph is another in the Kyle Pharmacy Series. It was posted on 11th August, 1931.

This stunning photograph, postmarked 16th February 1903, is simply marked 'Shieling, Isle of Skye'. In early summer, whole townships would be on the move with their stock of sheep, cattle and horses, during the annual migration to more luxuriant higher pastures. These provided lush and sweet grazing for the animals after the long winter months, and a welcome change of scenery for the tenantry with opportunities for more social occasions! Taking food and bedding with them, the first task would be to carry out any necessary repairs to the huts in order to make them habitable for the duration of the stay. While the precise time at the shieling evidently varied somewhat throughout the Highlands and Islands, the period from the beginning of May to mid-August is often associated with this annual event.

The British Fisheries Society established a port at Stein in 1787, but the venture did not prosper as planned and it failed to become another Ullapool. Perhaps because of these imposed and innovatory activities, Stein can claim fame on two other counts. It boasts Skye's oldest inn, situated in the line of buildings strung out around the bay, and the survey for the first ever road in Skye, running from the the village to Dunvegan, Bracadale and Broadford was commenced about 1799.

STEIN, WATERNISH, SKYE.

A long way from home, the Channel Fleet no doubt caused a stir when it anchored in Loch Bay – and perhaps for some, brought back memories of the crofter rebellion twenty years earlier, when marines were despatched to North Skye. This card is postmarked Waternish, June 1907.

A big house, abandoned and gradually falling into ruin, is a sad spectacle, and even though it was many years ago I still recall the sense of shock I felt at my first glimpse of Waternish House. Its best remembered owner was Captain Macdonald, a Victorian naturalist and keen sportsman who had served during the Crimean War. Most writers agree that he certainly had a way with animals and birds when he wasn't actually shooting them around his estate. His otter hounds were famous, while the lawns and pond near the house provided an apparently harmonious sanctuary for all manner of species – rabbits, a white hare, a fox, a tame seal, pet otters, a heron, wild duck, moorhens and a peregrine falcon with clipped wings. A tame hind followed him everywhere, and on one occasion when the Captain was visiting a warship in the bay, the hind startled the crew by swimming around the boat in an effort to find its master!

Norman Magnus MacLeod, 1839-1929, the 26th Chief of the Clan, photographed on the tower at Dunvegan Castle c1910. The wearing of eagle's feathers denotes his status as Chief.

The island's most famous building, Dunvegan Castle. The renowned treasures housed here, in walls sometimes up to eleven feet in thickness, almost demand a small book of their own. There are Jacobite relics, charters, documents and letters from Samuel Johnson, and Sir Walter Scott. The star attractions are the Dunvegan cup (possibly a chalice) made of wood and silver, bearing the date 1493, Rory Mor's Drinking Horn and, of course, the Fairy Flag. The latter is a ragged piece of faded silk which was gifted by a fairy to a previous Chief, or obtained from the Middle East during the Crusades – take your pick! In any event it is said that on the occasions it has been unfurled a crisis has been averted and the Clan saved.

Dunvegan Castle. East Front

6990. Dunvegan Village from the Golf Course, Isle of Skye.

These two photographs, above and right, both taken from the golf course, show Dunvegan village from slightly different angles, with the Cuillins in the distance making an impressive backdrop. The panorama created by the two pictures emphasises the scattered nature of the community, while the well cultivated croftland and smartly maintained buildings give a general air of prosperity.

DUNVEGAN THE PIER AND BAY, SKYE

Posted from the village on 23rd July 1937, the message on this card reads: 'We found nice rooms just outside the village at 'Millburn'. At the moment we are writing in the P.O. It was a marvellous ride over the hills – hardly a house all the way.' The SS *Hebrides*, moored at the pier, provided a lifeline to small, remote communities such as Dunvegan.

Dunvegan Village looking towards the Cuillins, Isle of Skye.

Kilmuir Church and Macleod's Tables

The roofless church at Kilmuir and its burial ground provide the last resting place for some of the Chiefs of the Dunvegan MacLeods. On one of the walls left standing, there is a memorial providing a particularly poignant reminder of the Great War. In 1915, at the age of twenty one, Iain Breac MacLeod was killed in France while serving with the Black Watch; he was the last male heir of the line. The stone memorial on the left of the picture was erected by Simon Lord Lovat over the grave of his father, whose death occurred while on a visit to the castle. In the background are those two flat topped mountains, Healabhal Mhor and Healabhal Beag, known as MacLeod's Tables.

Top A little group stand at the entrance of the Dunvegan Hotel, c1910. This was a Temperance Hotel until 1947 when Flora, Mrs MacLeod of MacLeod, successfully urged the licensing court to grant a licence, against the wishes of the majority living in the locality. However, nearly fifty years later, I doubt that there are too many complaints!

Above The Mill, Glendale, c1914. Glendale is another district in Skye which seems to have an identity and character all of its own, although this is perhaps not surprising considering its isolated location in the far north-west of the island, where it is situated on the far side of an enormous hill. For these reasons, everything came in and departed from the village by steamer at one time, using the pier at Loch Pooltiel. The mill was an asset of some local significance; self-sufficiency where possible was not merely desirable, but a necessity.

POOLTIEL BAY, GLENDALE, SKYE.

The gates of Hamara Lodge at Glendale. Now derelict, Hamara should have had its place in history, but it was not to be. During the Glendale crofter rebellion of 1882-3 it was intended that the lodge should be requisitioned by a posse of five policemen, but they were never allowed to reach it, and were subsequently run off the island! All the ingredients for a clash were present: an insensitive landlord imposing petty restrictions; illegal retaliatory action by the crofters in seizing Waterstein sheep farm; the issuance of writs which remained unserved; the gunboat HMS *Jackal* in the Loch; and the voluntary surrender of the ringleaders, followed by sixty one days imprisonment in Calton Jail, Edinburgh. As a result of these events, John MacPherson, the Milovaig crofter, helped to gain a Royal Commission which resulted in the Crofters' Holdings Act of 1886. Not for nothing is he recalled as 'The Glendale Martyr.'

Borrodale School in Glendale is thought to have opened in 1877, although the earliest extant logbook is for 1904, at which time 102 pupils were recorded as attending. Numbers increased to 120 in 1920 but dropped to only 25 at the end of the Second World War. They continue to fluctuate at around this level. Borrodale Primary School is now the only school in the district, with both Borreraig and Colbost Schools having closed in the last 30 years.

62   POST-OIFIG POLTIEL AGUS CAMUS GHLINN-DÀIL.

Glendale Post Office, (circa 1905). The parish of Duirinish, north-west of Dunvegan, was a comparatively well populated district in mid-Victorian times. The Post Office established a receiving office here in 1855, linked by foot runners with an office in Dunvegan. This was upgraded to a horse post in 1890.

Poolbiel Bay and Pier, Glendale, Skye

Pooltiel pier is quiet and deserted now, a place of memories, but if any one area of Glendale could have been described as the hub of activity, this was surely it! The arrival of any boat at any of the piers in these often remote communities was a highly significant event. Regular callers such as the *Dunara Castle* or the *Hebrides* brought cargo, mail, cattle, passengers and above all, news of the outside world. A blast on the siren as the boat rounded the headland was sufficient to turn a previously deserted pierhead into quite a throng in minutes, as people made their way there to await her docking.

If you close your eyes and breathe in, you can almost smell the luxuriant vegetation and the newly cut hay in this picture of a croft in high summer. Sixty-five years ago when the photograph was taken, you would probably have heard, in the surrounding croftland, that shy and elusive bird, more often heard than seen, the corncrake. Now more or less confined to the Outer Isles, where traditional agricultural practices are still encouraged, I suspect it is many a year since its distinctive cry was heard on Skye.

The cliffs around Waterstein Head and Neist Point, where the lighthouse is situated, are more than just dramatic. Spectacular would be a more appropriate adjective, and in a gale, awe-inspiring would not be out of place. There are fine views across The Little Minch towards the Uists, and in spells of calm weather there is a good chance of seeing dolphins and whales. This is the westernmost promontory of Skye, and prior to the building of the lighthouse in 1909 the dangerous reefs had claimed many ships – one even as the lighthouse was under construction. Eighty years later, on 14th December, 1989, the light was automated, the keepers withdrawn and redundant buildings sold. By 1998 all the lighthouses around our coasts will have suffered the same fate and a way of life will have vanished for ever. No longer will it be possible to get the latest intelligence from a keeper about shipping movements, bird migration, an instant weather forecast – or if very lucky, a mug of tea!

BRACADALE TO LUIB

There are numerous geological features of interest around the rocky coast of Loch Bracadale – cliffs, natural arches, caves and detached pillars of rock – all products of natural coastal erosion. Near Idrigill Point are these famous stacks, known as Macleod's Maidens, around which much folklore and many legends are woven. The largest rock, about two hundred feet high, is known as the Mother; the smaller, her daughters, the Maidens. When seen from certain angles, some claim to see a likeness to Queen Victoria in the larger stack.

The original property on the site of the Orbost Hotel appears to have been a tack house in the eighteenth century. At that time, Orbost could boast a school and township of some size. That was, of course, before the Clearances came, and the population transported, *en bloc*, eventually to found a new township of the same name on the Snowy River in Victoria, Australia. This early 1930s photograph shows the house during the period when it was in use as an hotel. In more recent years it was the home of the late Otta Swire, a leading writer on the legends and folklore of the island.

To cater for the increasing demands of tourists in the years following the Great War, many small boarding houses and bed and breakfast establishments, like the Argyle Boarding House pictured here, sprung up on Skye. In many cases, the extra seasonal income from tourism supplemented what could be made from the more traditional crofting activities.

More or less equidistant between Dunvegan and Harlosh, at a point where several roads meet, lies the small township of Roskhill. Between 1917 and 1937 its Post Office was known as 'Harlosh'. Quite properly, the name reverted to Roskhill when a new office was opened in the neighbouring village of Harlosh itself in March 1937, and this photograph dates from around the time of the change.

Ullinish Lodge is situated in a hollow of the moor between the road and the loch at Bracadale. Writing in his journal, James Boswell records that he and Dr. Samuel Johnson reached here on 21st September 1773, to find 'a very good farmhouse of two stories, a plentiful garden (a great rarity in Skye), and several trees.' They spent an agreeable two days being shown the sights of the neighbourhood. In 1950, a visitor to the Lodge, now an hotel, wrote: 'This is our home for tonight – an old shooting lodge on the shores of Loch Bracadale – and looking towards the Uist islands of the Hebrides, just visible on the horizon. Wonderful sunset over the loch tonight and now full moon showing up the Coolins.'

Sorting the lambs, Bracadale. Here, the hills are alive, not with the sound of music, but with the bleating of sheep and lambs. This is a nicely pictured scene at the sheep fank.

A trio of shepherds with their sticks, a dog and two lambs. It would be interesting to hear whether any of these men recognise themselves, or are known to others.

Planting potatoes. During the mid nineteenth century, the entire potato crop failed on all too many occasions, either due to successive bad winters or blight. The year 1846 is noteworthy for widespread deprivation and famine, followed by the subsequent ravaging effects of disease – cholera, scurvy and typhus – which produced scenes on Skye that have become all too familiar in Africa in recent years. An essential ingredient of an already restricted diet, potatoes were gown an almost every croft. This photograph of 1900 shows the planting underway in soil freshly turned with the cas chrom, and fertilised with seaweed from the shore.

Casting peats, c1900. The laying in of fuel was both essential and very hard work, often carried out at the peat moss in family groups. Once the topmost layer of vegetation had been skimmed off, the cutter would work a narrow strip using a toirsgian, the wooden spade in use in most, but not all, parts of Skye at this time. The cut peat would then be thrown, and left higgledy-piggledy on the moor to dry, prior to being stacked. It is said that when dry the blackest peats burn the brightest.

At Drynoch, the old Automobile Association signpost on the A863 main road points the way to Dunvegan via Bracadale, and to Sligachan through the Glen. However, our route to Carbost lies downhill, and around the head of Loch Harport in the middle distance.

Below and Bottom Opposite Two comprehensive turn of the century views of the buildings on the southern shore of Loch Harport which comprised Skye's only distillery, the Talisker Distillery at Carbost. The business takes its name from the big house about five miles distant, and the amber nectar has been produced here more or less continuously since the brothers Hugh and Kenneth MacAskill founded the business in 1830 – that is, apart from interruptions during the Second World War, and between 1960-62 when there was a disastrous fire. Now part of the giant United Distillers group (Guinness Plc), spirit distilled here goes for both blending, and single malt whisky. Malted barley, water and yeast come together to produce the famous Talisker single malt which has a distinctive peaty taste influenced by the local water drawn from a source above the village. The Visitor Centre apart, there are sixteen full time employees. Annual production was forty thousand gallons of spirit at the time these photographs were taken in 1901.

In 1900, a pier and tramway were built at Carbost to serve the distillery. Small steamers known as puffers brought in barley and returned to the mainland with wooden casks filled with malt whisky. Indeed, both barley and coal were still coming in this way until the late sixties when, owing to the general improvement in roads, the practice ceased. By 1990, United Distillers had declared the pier to be surplus to their requirements. This picture shows the SS *Dunara Castle*, a regular visitor to Carbost. Between 1875 and 1948 she played an essential role in island life – a true 'Hebridean institution'.

'Sunday best for the photographer' was plainly the order of the day for this little group of children pictured alongside the Free Church in Carbost. The sender of the postcard identified their names in manuscript before posting it on 9th January, 1911.

Another charming study, this time of Trein Burn.

The message on this card, postmarked 9th July 1945, reads 'Was in a local pub yesterday called the Tighe Clachain and said to an old boy, "Does it always rain like this around here?" He replied, "AW NAW, IT SNAWS SOMETEEMS"!!'

Glen Brittle House, a former MacLeod shooting lodge, is the most substantial building in the glen of the same name. Prior to 1914 it was taken for the season by such eminent climbers as Professor Norman Collie, and although many tourists never find their way into this remote and sparsely populated place, it is a Mecca for climbers intent on making assaults on the southern hills in the Cuillin range. Accommodation here has always been very limited, and early climbers recall with affection the homely comforts provided by the Chisholms at the Post Office, the Campbells at the Cottage and the Macraes at the Farm. From 1931, the latter took a lease on the Lodge and let it to climbers. On another postcard dated 3rd August 1926 quoting the sender's address as c/o Mrs Macrae, Glen Brittle, is an intriguing message: 'Here safely, good weather and jolly company. I cannot remember the name of the tailor in Station Road who made a climbing suit for me. I want to ask him to repeat the knickers (green corduroy) as nearly as possible and as speedily as possible. They were destroyed in the train fire and my second line is rather weak! I don't suppose they will be in time to come here, but he can get on with it.'

Ninety years ago, Portnalong and Fiscavaig consisted of a mere handful of dwellings, but all that changed about 1920 when the Board of Agriculture purchased this MacLeod land in order to establish small-holdings for an influx of settlers from Scalpay and Harris. Indeed, when a few existing Skye families were removed to the mainland to assist in these arrangements, some hinted suspiciously that the Board was experimenting in eugenics. This resettlement at Portnalong created about seventy new dwellings, and the incomers were quick to realise the potential of selling hand-made tweed to visitors. Sending for the spinning wheels and hand looms they had originally left behind in Harris, the new settlers soon established a tweed industry at Portnalong. This quickly became the centre for cloth sold under the trade name of Portnaskye tweed. Until the Second World War, the annual production was sold in late August at a Fèill or Gathering, and in 1930 one visitor recorded seeing 'the most beautiful hues of wool I have ever set eyes upon'. This picture and the four opposite show some of the stages of tweed production.

Simply entitled 'Crofters' Cottages, Isle of Skye', this is a photograph from the late 1920s.

PACKING THE WOOL AT PORTNALONG, SKYE

DYEING THE WOOL AT PORTNALONG, SKYE

MAKING THE TWEED AT PORTNALONG, SKYE

Rising steeply in places and continually twisting and turning, the only road skirts the head of Loch Slapin, runs beneath rugged Blaven, and after passing through Kilmarie and rounding the shoulder of Ben Meabost, finally reaches Elgol with, one feels, almost a sense of achievement and relief. Before the coming of the road, the natural way to have reached this small isolated community would have been by boat. Today, the population numbers some 135 people.

A post office, a sub office to Broadford, was first opened in the township of Elgol in 1880.

At one time, the community of Elgol depended entirely on crofting and a little fishing for its livelihood, although after the Great War things began to change as motor transport became more popular. More establishments were converted to cater for the increasing numbers of tourists, who had been visiting since Victorian times. People came to savour the stupendous views, visit nearby Spar Cave, and to take the boat trip down Loch Scavaig to see famed Loch Coruisk – an almost obligatory item on every travel itinerary. As long ago as 1831 J.M.W. Turner himself had visited and painted the loch.

Elgol Village, c1930. The road twists like a corkscrew through this crofting township as it rises to the top of the hill, in the left of the picture, before commencing its steep descent to the shore.

THE GRAND VIEW TEA ROOMS. ELGOL. SKYE

The Grand View tea rooms in Elgol – once a welcome find for tourists, no doubt! If views were to be graded in the same way as listed buildings, then this would be a Grade I example, with the shapely cone of Gars Bheinn (2934 feet high) rising straight from the sea in the background and terminating the Cuillin ridge at this point. The little wooden telephone hut on the right provided a much needed communication link with the island of Soay, three and a half miles distant, and just out of the picture. The postmistress there used the facility only for the transmission of telegrams. At the turn of the century, possible medical emergencies were the cause of much concern to the islanders; in the event of a crisis, it was first necessary to make the six mile journey by motor boat into Loch Brittle, then undertake a nine mile trek overland through the Glen to reach the telegraph office at Carbost. The doctor, who at that time resided at Struan, on Loch Bracadale, could then finally be raised.

This picture of Elgol was taken long before a jetty was built, and instead of being moored, boats are pulled up on the shore. The substantial building at sea level, surrounded by a wall and overlooking Loch Scavaig, is the school. From the hill, the road descends steeply to the shore by a 1 in 3.5 gradient, and in the earlier days of motoring, cars that had made the descent were unable, on occasions, to complete their return journey without the assistance of cart horses.

The sea is choppy on this misty day, and in such weather conditions the lady seated in the boat is more likely to be making a necessary journey to the island of Soay, than taking the tourist route down Loch Scavaig to Loch Coruisk.

A MacBrayne steamer, the *Glencoe,* on one of her Loch Scavaig excursions in the years immediately preceding the Great War.

Passengers leaving Loch Scavaig. Here, near the landing place, the salt water of Loch Scavaig meets the fresh water of Loch Coruisk. The Loch lies hidden from view, a short scramble away over the rocks.

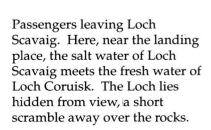

THE CIOCH OF SGUMAIN, SKYE.   Copyright

The Cuillins are a group of mountains without parallel in Britain. In the mid-nineteenth century, the remoter peaks were thought to be inaccessible, but through the determination of the early pioneering climbers, the heights were conquered one by one. The gabbro rock and beautiful corries provided a paradise for the climber and cragsman, many of whom claimed that the Alps and the Dolomites offered nothing more sporting. Sgurr Sgumain is a peak 3104 feet high; the Cioch a rocky outcrop, as this dramatic picture shows. The first recorded ascent of the Cioch was made in 1906 by Norman Collie, a Professor of Organic Chemistry, and John Mackenzie of Sconser, who, over a period of forty years, forged a unique partnership with Collie and became renowned far beyond these shores as the pre-eminent Cuillin guide.

At a height of 3206 feet, Sgurr Dearg (The Red Peak) is fairly easily reached from Glen Brittle. For climbers, however, the pinnacle is an 'optional extra'. It stands out from the peak by some twenty feet, a solitary column of rock sometimes referred to as the Old Man of Skye. It was considered to be inaccessible until 18th August 1880, when the Pilkington brothers (of glass manufacturing fame) made the first recorded ascent. However, at some previous date, John Mackenzie is thought to have climbed the peak. Later, he accompanied the brothers on a further successful attempt when they again conquered the pinnacle by a different route – another 'first'.

At the summit of Sgurr na Banachdich (3167 feet), three climbers regain their breath after the ascent, and admire the view of the surrounding peaks. This mountain, like many others, has a variety of local names, including 'Hill of the Milkmaid', originating perhaps from the ruins of the shielings to be seen in the corrie, out of sight below.

This fine view is taken from the summit of Bruach-na-Frithe (3143 feet). Splintered, shattered peaks, terraces, and knife-like ridges abound. The Cuillins, it is said, exercise a magnetic attraction not only on climbers, but also their compass needles, so beware!

A well-equipped little group having a break for refreshment (and perhaps a drop of the Talisker!) somewhere in the Cuillins. The exact spot is not mentioned, but I am tempted to suggest a location for this picture – Coire na Creiche, with Waterpipe Gully in the background. This area (if indeed I am correct) was the venue for one of the most savage Clan clashes in 1601. It took place between the MacLeods and the MacDonalds, the latter being the overwhelming victors on this occasion, and was the last altercation between the two clans. James VI, concerned for his reputation in London, brought the warring factions together in amity, which has endured to the present day.

For many years Sgurr-nan-Gillean (The Pinnacle Ridge) was considered to be the highest peak in the Cuillins, although at a confirmed height of 3167 feet it is in fact equal fifth with Sgurr na Banachdich. Professor J.D. Forbes made the first recorded ascent in July 1836, while John Mackenzie, born in 1856, successfully conquered the ridge at the tender age of ten. The mountain is more commonly viewed as a backcloth to the Sligachan Inn, but this picture is taken from Sgurr a'Bhasteir. During the Second World War, commando units underwent training here, under the experienced eyes of mountaineers familiar with the terrain.

Blaven from Sgurr nan Gillean, Isle of Skye.

Footprints in the snow and a carefully placed ice axe tell the story: the climber who took this photograph had had an exhilarating climb to the top of Sgurr na Gillean on a day of excellent visibility, before recording the scene with his camera. Glen Sligachan, far below, divides the Black Cuillin – where our photographer stands – from the Red Hills in the distance. The magnificent outline of Blaven (3042 feet) forms the centre of the skyline of this picture.

These days, Sligachan and Glen Brittle probably share the honours just about equally for the title 'mountaineering centre of Skye'. At Sligachan, roads meet but there is no village – just the famous Inn, shown here in this 1902 photograph. Marsco (2414 feet), with its distinctive sloping ridge, lies immediately behind, further up the Glen. It is said that a mile of walking in Glen Sligachan is the equivalent of two ordinary miles, such is the ruggedness of the terrain.

This superb card, postmarked 3rd August 1910, shows the Sligachan Inn with Sgurr nan Gillean under snow. In his 1933 book, *Tramping in Skye*, B.H. Humble aptly describes the Inn: 'If one arrives at noon the place seems deserted. No one remains indoors at Sligachan. Towards evening the different parties will come straggling back: cheery cragsmen after a day testing their powers in the gullies and on the ridges; trampers who have kept to the glens and lesser hills; an artist maybe, who has failed – as many others have failed before him – to put Coruisk on to canvas; and fishermen, with or without their trout or salmon. But all have mighty appetites!'

Sligichan Inn and Sgurr-na-Gillean. Skye.

Above Season after season from 1886 onwards, Professor Norman Collie returned to the Inn at Sligachan to mount climbing expeditions, assisted by his friend John Mackenzie. The latter's knowledge of the mountains was unrivalled, and he was variously described as 'a capital climber', 'a perfect gentleman' and 'a charming and delightful companion' – as the Sligachan Visitors' Book testifies. Yet, the class riven nature of society at the turn of the century made it impossible for the Professor to invite his friend back to the bar at the Inn after a day's climbing together on the hills. Instead, Mackenzie had to trudge the three miles back to his croft at Sconser. He died in 1933, aged 76, and was buried at Struan. Collie made arrangements for his headstone. About this time, Collie himself gave up active climbing and retired to the Inn (now an hotel), accompanied only by memories of his previous achievements. Nine years later, in 1942, he too died, joining his friend in the old burying ground at Struan, where their graves lie side by side. They had been foremost in opening up the Cuillins, and both have mountains named after them.

Opposite Bottom The Sconser Hotel, previously a shooting lodge on the MacDonald deer forest, was built on the site of the inn visited by Johnson and Boswell in 1773. However, of much greater significance was a meeting which took place here in 1745 between the Chiefs of MacLeod and MacDonald, who had been requested to throw their weight behind Prince Charles Edward Stuart's bid for the throne. For the most part, Skye's sympathies lay with the Jacobites, but in fact the Chiefs refused to declare themselves for the Prince. Some speculate that had a different decision been taken, it would have been enough to tip the scales, and his eventual defeat at Culloden could have been avoided. Had this happened, then the entire course of history would have been altered in two continents – an interesting thought for conjecture and argument.

Glamaig (2537 feet) photographed in 1920. In 1899 a truly extraordinary event took place here which has its own very special niche in the history of Sligachan. A Gurkha soldier, Halvidar Harkabir Thapa, known as Herkia, ran non-stop from the bridge outside the Inn to the summit of Glamaig and back in just fifty five minutes. On the descent he encountered much loose scree, and his achievement is all the more noteworthy for being accomplished barefoot. Most people would take twice fifty five minutes merely to reach the *base* of the mountain. This never likely to be repeated feat is confirmed by an entry in the Scottish Mountaineering Club Guide, but for those seeking more information may I suggest reference to Alasdair Alpin MacGregor's *Skye and the Inner Hebrides*, published in 1953.

6870 A Township midst the Mountains of Skye.

'A township midst the mountains' is an apt description for Luib, whose name comes from the Gaelic word meaning a bend. The township nestles on either side of a curve in the Sligachan to Broadford road, which travels around the shore of Loch Ainort. Mountains dominate the landward side, while across a channel half a mile wide lies the island of Scalpay.

Luib, Isle of Skye.

Certainly until well after the Second World War, the township of Luib was considered to be one of the most picturesque in the whole island, and one of the 'sights' to see, with virtually every house beautifully thatched. Such buildings as remain are now mostly slated, and for today's visitors there is a Folk Museum, complete with peat fire.

STRATH AND SLEAT

Clach Glas, often called 'The Matterhorn of Skye', is a great rock tower 2590 feet high. It forms part of the Blaven ridge, located near the head of Loch Slapin, west of Broadford. The rock of Clach Glas consists of coarse crystalline gabbro, and is quite different from the nearby Red Hills whose granite forms are more rounded in shape.

66. The Coolins, Black and Red, from Clach Glas, Skye.

For the climber, this panorama is one of the most rewarding Skye views – the Black Cuillin ridge in the distance, with the Red Hills dominating the middle and right foreground.

The picturesque and scattered township of Torrin lies along the shore of Loch Slapin in the parish of Strath. A visitor to the School House in July 1937 was moved to write: 'This is a wonderful place and I wish I could describe the colours. Fuchsia and iris are growing wild, and a lot of wild flowers, the names of which I do not know'. The ridge of Blaven (3042 feet), with its cleft and magnificently rugged head, completes the picture.

Ben Blaven from Torrin, c1875. The bizarre case of a small island off the coast of Skye being given away as a prize on a German TV show recently, serves to highlight the unsatisfactory nature of land ownership and transfer in Scotland. Indeed, secrecy over ownership – which is often hidden behind nominee companies registered abroad – coupled with absentee landlords with no interest in their property other than to minimise tax, have long created suspicions and genuine concerns among those whose living depends on the land. Happily, no such problems arose here. In 1991, the much respected John Muir Trust negotiated the purchase of the 5200 acre crofting estate of Torrin, and the area is now being managed jointly with the local community.

Blaven and Loch Slapin from Torrin Village, with the Post Office in the foreground, photographed in the late twenties. A sub office, under Broadford, was first established in the township in 1898.

The slopes of Beinn an Dubhaich, located south of Broadford in the hills around Suardal and Kilchrist, yielded sporadic and small quantities of marble throughout the nineteenth century. Those with a little imagination and a keen eye will still find traces of the small railway line, opened about 1904, which ran from Broadford pier through the glen to Kilbride, where the quarries and crushing equipment were located. The line continued to Kilchrist, where quarrying also took place, together with cutting and polishing.

Skye Marble Ltd. was formed in 1907 and skilled Belgian workers were brought in by the company, although financial and external problems resulted in its closure only six years later. Nevertheless, marble quarried here was used for the high altar at Iona Abbey, and is also found in Hamilton Palace and Armadale Castle – and probably in the building of the Old Manse at Strath. The Vatican and the Palace of Versailles are thought, traditionally, to have received pieces too. These pictures show various quarrying operations underway, including a train crossing the Broadford river and the workers' complex up in the hills.

The locomotive 'Skylark', seen here near Campbell's Hotel at Broadford Pier in 1911, was used for bringing the marble down from the glen before it was loaded aboard ships and taken away by sea. (Picture reproduced here by kind permission of John J. Patience).

Old Broadford Church, more usually called Kilchrist Church, has not seen a conventional church service for 150 years. The ivy covered ruins lie alongside the Broadford to Elgol road, next to the ancient burying ground of the MacKinnons. The few stones that remain of Corrie Chatachan, the MacKinnon house where Johnson and Boswell received so much hospitality on two occasions during their 'tour' of 1773, may still be seen a mile and a half away, across the Broadford River in the shadow of Beinn na Caillich.

This turn of the century view shows Broadford from the Torrin road. The Broadford Hotel is visible on the right of the bridge.

Broadford Hotel is the original home of the world famous Drambuie liqueur, and at about the time this photograph was taken in 1902, James Ross, who ran the hotel, was making the whisky-based liqueur on the premises. From the nearby pier, MacBrayne steamers took supplies away, ultimately destined for places as far apart as the Continent and even Australia. Ross registered the Drambuie name in 1893, having been handed down the secret recipe by his father, who had in turn received it from the MacKinnon family of Strath. They acquired the recipe from a grateful supporter of Prince Charles Edward Stuart, in recognition of the crucial part played by that Clan in aiding his final escape from Skye in 1746. Even today, each bottle of Drambuie, alas no longer produced in Broadford, still proclaims the Prince's name – an enduring link with the '45.

Broadford has an impressive setting, and its houses are dotted on moorland which encircles a wide curving bay, overlooked by the familiar shape of Beinn na Caillich, 2400 feet high. But the township is geographically important as well as picturesque, as virtually all roads in the area pass through it.   Broadford 'proper' is the area around this bridge where roads meet, and the hotel, bank, post office and hospital are all situated.

Together, the Bank of Scotland and the Post Office make up Broadford's financial centre. On the view showing the bridge, it is clear that the Post Office has not yet been built. Now, however, a smart new building has appeared and perhaps, the person standing in the doorway is none other than Mr. MacInnes himself.

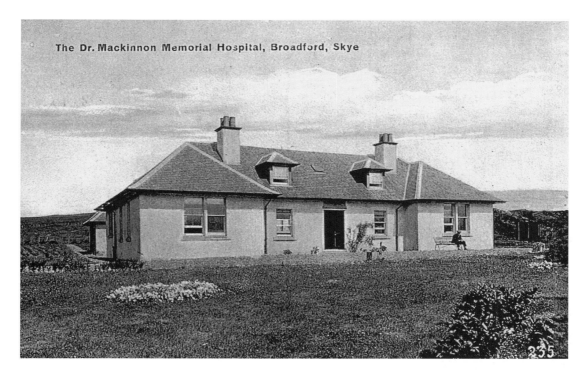

The Dr. Mackinnon Memorial Hospital, Broadford, Skye

Top This hospital was founded as a memorial to the Reverend Donald MacKinnon, who died in 1888. He was the last of several generations of his family who had been successive Ministers of the Parish of Strath. First opened in 1914 as a four bed cottage hospital, this photograph shows the original building. Subsequent enlargement provided eight beds in two wards, a small operating theatre, X-ray apparatus (housed in an outbuilding), staff accommodation, a kitchen and a small laundry. The present building dates largely from 1963. Nowadays, this twenty-eight bed general hospital provides medical care not only for Skye, but also for part of the adjacent mainland.

Above Campbell's Hotel would be the first building to be encountered by travellers as they stepped off the MacBrayne steamer at Broadford Pier. Hotels, conveniently sited like this one, were popular with tourists as the state of the tide sometimes led to very late evening arrivals – or demanded early morning departures. A number of obviously interested people are watching the photographer at work as he takes this picture, c1905.

In this slightly earlier view, Campbell's Hotel – then a much smaller building – is also visible.

A paddle steamer at the head of Broadford pier. Before the First World War, when this picture was taken, puffers (small vessels with shallow draughts) also delivered bulky cargoes such as coal to Broadford. Until the 1939-45 War, the Portree steamer made a morning and evening call at the pier. But times were changing, and improved roads combined with the increasing use of motor transport meant that Broadford could be reached relatively easily from Kyleakin and the Kyle ferry. When it came to the financial choice of developing either Armadale pier or the one at Broadford, the latter lost out, and was allowed to fall into disrepair.

Broadford school, c1908.

Some school children, and the proud owner of this Aberdeen registered Austin 7, look towards the camera in this scene outside Broadford School. The date of the photograph is within three years of the car's 1932 registration date.

Near the Harrapool Stores (proprietor Mr. D. Campbell) is the Waterloo area of Broadford, so called because at one time a large number of retired soldiers from Wellington's army resided there. It is believed that upwards of fifteen hundred men from Skye fought at the Battle of Waterloo in 1815.

Entitled 'An Old Highland Cottage, Broadford', this picture was taken by Miss M.E.M. Donaldson (1876-1958). Known more simply as M.E.M.D. or 'Herself', Miss Donaldson wrote a number of books on the history and traditions of the Western Highlands and Islands. When not engaged upon these, she was either photographing in the field with a large amount of cumbersome photographic equipment, or supervising the building of her own house (using traditional materials), at Sanna Bheag, in Ardnamurchan.

When this card was posted in 1904, peat carrying was a common sight throughout the Isles, and was a task that was very much regarded as being reserved for women. The baskets were usually made of either hazel or willow.

This extraordinary milestone, photographed here in the 1930s, must have brought a smile to the face of many who noticed it by the roadside. Surely unofficial, it proclaimed, maybe, the indisputable fact that Skye is a long way from London, and that 'we go about matters in our own way up here'. However, there may be another explanation. Marble Arch replaced an earlier brick gateway, known as Cumberland Gate, and named in memory of a Duke of the same name. He had fought a famous battle on Drummossie Muir in 1746 which had earned him the nick-name 'The Butcher of Culloden'. Perhaps, then, this milestone was a subtle and coded message to the English!

Breakish School from N. W.

The pupils of Breakish School pose for this 1909 photograph. Sixty-five years later, in 1974, and before their move to Broadford, the Old School was the headquarters of the West Highland Publishing Company. They, of course, publish the radical newspaper the *West Highland Free Press*, which started from humble origins in nearby Kyleakin in 1972. Now well established, the paper is eagerly read every week throughout the Western Isles, Skye and Lochalsh, and far beyond.

Ashaig (Broadford) Airstrip, built by army engineers newly returned from Far Eastern postings, was completed in time for Loganair's newly scheduled 1972 services linking Skye with Glasgow and Inverness. But two years later, the world oil crisis resulted in modifications to flight schedules, leaving only the Glasgow link intact, and sadly, low passenger usage caused the service to be withdrawn entirely on 25th March 1988. This picture, taken by the author, shows a Britten-Norman Mk 111-2 Trislander G-BDOS, inward bound from Glasgow, landing at Ashaig on 17th October 1980.

This picture shows the Quern or handmill, used for grinding corn, in action. Two millstones were set one above the other, and grain was poured into a hole at the centre of the upper one. The woman then revolved this with the aid of a stick, the action often being accompanied by a Gaelic chant. This is a George Washington Wilson photograph, c1890.

The lighthouse, Kyleakin, 1925. The Commissioners of Northern Lighthouses first lit the lamp here in 1857, and the station was manned until 1960. Subsequently, the lighthouse cottages (duly renovated, and with the newly created forty foot long Long Room) became the last home of author Gavin Maxwell (1914-1969), who acquired them in 1964. He had plans to establish various wildlife projects around his home, but these failed to come to fruition due to his untimely death at the age of fifty five. A gifted writer, his best selling title *Ring of Bright Water* told the story of his Shangri-La which he called Camusfeàrna (The Bay of Alders), situated at nearby Sandaig. Teko, the last of his famous otters, died three months after his master, and is buried on the lighthouse island.

THE LIGHTHOUSE, KYLEAKIN, SKYE.

Even a cursory glance at this picture reveals that it is not Kyleakin at all, but a scene at the Old Ferry Pier at Kyle – a mistake which was subsequently corrected by the publishers. At one time, vast herds of cattle were driven along the old 'green' droving roads and passes to Kylerhea, there to be made to swim across the fast flowing currents to the mainland. In this 1927 picture, wide flat bottomed boats, known at garboards, are being used to carry the cattle across the narrows from Kyleakin in safety.

A HIGHLAND CARGO, KYLEAKIN, SKYE.

Kyle of Lochalsh lies just over the water from Kyleakin, and Alexander Smith was waiting there to cross to Skye in 1864: 'The ferry is a narrow passage between the mainland and Skye; the current is powerful there, difficult to pull against on gusty days; and the ferrymen are loath to make the attempt unless well remunerated'. However, after receiving a thorough drenching in the open boat, which gave him the excuse to warm himself with 'a caulker of Glenlivet', he and his companions eventually reached the safety of the Inn at Kyleakin. They had crossed the 'doorstep' to Skye.

Top In order to transport vehicles over the water to and from Kyle of Lochalsh, cars had to be mounted across a boat on two planks of wood, their wheels suitably secured with chocks on either side, and made fast with ropes through the spokes. If sea conditions permitted, men using long oars would row the boat across the narrows. In the early days the fee was £1. I believe it was unknown for a car to slip off, but on the odd, very rare occasion, a vehicle might be ditched deliberately in mid-channel in order to prevent a boat from capsizing. The ferrymen knew their job well.

Above The ramps are lowered, and the clang of metal on stone announces the arrival of the ferry boat at Kyleakin, bringing the bakers' van from Kyle for a round of deliveries. The design of the boat has been improved; now there is a turntable to bring the single vehicle on to the jetty. In the background is Castle Maoil, a gaunt ruined keep with walls eleven feet thick, and Skye's best known landmark. A stronghold of the MacKinnon Clan Chiefs between 1490 and 1610, the structure, having been ravaged by the elements for many years, is now in the care of Skye and Lochalsh District Council.

This peaceful scene dates from 1952. The *Loch Etive Queen* is moored at the quayside opposite the White Heather Cafe, and the ferry boat lies at the pierhead. However, the atmosphere was far from peaceful when the first ever Sunday sailing of the boat to Skye was made in June 1965, amid strong protests. Many saw it as a desecration of the Sabbath, always strongly observed in the isles. One Free Church Minister, the Rev. Angus Smith, lay down on the jetty and was promptly arrested.

Posted in August 1920, this card carries the message: 'I do hope that next year you will come and sample this comfortable little Highland Inn at this jolly unsophisticated place. But do see Barrie's *Mary Rose* first'.

The Obbe (a word meaning tidal inlet or bay) is shown here in this 1902 Kyleakin picture.

The Duke and Duchess of York, later King George VI and Queen Elizabeth, arrived on Skye for a Royal Visit on 11th September 1933, which was declared a public holiday. They had journeyed by train to Kyle Station, where at the adjoining railway pier they were piped aboard a motor launch which took them to the yacht *Golden Hind*. The weather was glorious, and the Duchess was later credited with having used the words 'Skye-blue' for the first time. In this picture, the royal visitors (now at Kyleakin) are being welcomed by local dignitaries, including Cameron of Lochiel and the late Lord Macdonald (second left). Their Royal Highnesses went on to make a memorable visit to Dunvegan Castle, and to open the Elgin Hostel for Boys, in Portree.

When completed, the new bridge will effectively bypass Kyleakin, bringing the road to Skye's only roundabout, adjacent to Kyle House (left, and just out of sight in this photograph of 1930). This curious meandering inlet, an arm of the sea, is a real local asset, providing a delightfully sheltered area for plant and bird life, and a short but pleasant walk. Hopefully, it will survive future environmental pressures, and will be fully protected and even enhanced – but only in the best possible way for the benefit of local people and visitors alike.

It is said that Lord Macdonald built the island's first shop in Kyleakin about 1800, but he had other ambitious ideas too, including the building of a model village. In fact, a sizeable town was planned, and two storey houses with attics were designed for Kyleakin, which was to be renamed 'New Liverpool'. The project would have been a white elephant, and it is perhaps fortunate that his plans remained just plans.

Kyleakin Pier in 1909, with a paddle steamer approaching the wooden construction which is now only a memory. Originally built so that the P.S. *Glencoe* could make a stop here on her way to and from Kyle, the pier subsequently proved to be quite unsatisfactory at low tide and was removed.

These wide green verges were very much a feature of Kyleakin in its earlier days. The post office is visible second from the right in this picture, and although a receiving house for post was opened here in 1843, Kyleakin had to wait another thirty-eight years for its telegraph office. The group of ladies in the foreground is very likely on a day's outing to the Island.

Mr McPherson's general store, visible in the lower picture on the previous page, also doubled as the Post Office. (Detail from a photograph by Munro & Son of Dingwall, c1905).

At one time the King's Arms Hotel was owned by a certain Donald Skinner. He pioneered motor omnibus trips to the various places of interest around the island, and was what would be described today as an entrepreneur. In the days before telephones, and with literally an 'eye to business', he could sometimes be seen during the tourist season gazing through his telescope towards Kyle. There, displayed on a blackboard, he could see the number of passengers pre-booked for his tours, and was able to make his own plans accordingly before the visitors had even set foot on the island.

At Lusa Bridge, about four miles from Kyleakin, a narrow single track road begins a tortuous ascent through Glen Arroch before reaching a height of 911 feet at the top of the pass. Thereafter, it plunges dizzily downward to Kylerhea to meet the dangerous currents which race through the narrow channel dividing Skye from the mainland. This is the oldest of all the island's ferry crossing routes, and the views can be spectacular. In this 1930s photograph, Ian Neil Macpherson poses with his bicycle at the top of the pass for this picture, taken by his father, the well-known chemist from the Kyle Pharmacy.

Two hundred years ago, the former inn by the jetty would have been crowded with drovers, and all available space around the margins of the shore packed with bellowing cattle. Perhaps as many as eight thousand head of cattle annually were driven to this spot opposite the mainland, to be swum across when favourable water permitted. Secured by rope under the jaw to keep their heads above water, and tied head to tail in strings of eight, the cattle were preceded into the rushing torrent by the rowers and their helpers in the boats. Guided, encouraged and cajoled, they somehow made landfall on the Bernera shore opposite. What a sight it must have been! A re-enactment was unsuccessfully attempted some years ago. The old skills had been long forgotten and in any case, animal welfare organisations and public opinion would not, quite properly, allow such practices today.

509   KYLERHEA FERRY

'The ferryman takes advantage of an eddy tide moving near the shore in the opposite direction to the main tidal stream; he then at the right moment enters the main tidal river, crossing it diagonally. His skill lies in his exact knowledge of how far he must travel on the eddy tide; otherwise he would be swept down beyond the slip on the opposite side and would have difficulty in beating up to it against the full force of the main river'. So wrote Seton Gordon in *Afoot in the Hebrides*. Murdo MacKenzie, the then ferryman, retired in 1990 having operated the ferry for thirty-one years. He knew the tides well. The ferry still operates during the summer months.

Behind Broadford, a single track road strikes up over moorland and runs past the 'Black Lochs', making for Sleat. This is yet another very distinctive part of the island, known as 'The Garden of Skye', – 'a place of low hills, green fields, bird-haunted woods and sheltered shores'. Moorland gives way to a more wooded landscape near Kinloch; in spring the trees display soft pastel shades of green, while red berries and russet colours predominate in autumn. At all seasons, there are vistas of great beauty to be seen across the waters of the Sound towards the mainland. The picture is entitled 'Wandering Scottish Piper and Family'.

Kinloch Lodge, a former shooting lodge belonging to the Macdonald Estates, is situated on gently rising ground at the head of Loch na Dal. There has been a building on this site since 1540. Surrounded by woods, and once locally-famed gardens, of which traces still remain, the area was designated a Site of Special Scientific Interest some years ago. Since 1973, Lord Macdonald and his wife, Claire (a well-known writer on cookery matters), have created a small, comfortable hotel which has received international recognition. Kinloch Lodge was enlarged ten years later when it also became the Macdonald family home. This photograph was taken by the author in 1980 before the building was altered.

Duisdale House, now an hotel, is surrounded by rich gardens and wooded policies and enjoys a commanding view over the Sound of Sleat. For generations a family of MacKinnons had acted as standard bearers to the Macdonalds of Sleat, and was enfeoffed at Duisdalebeg for its services. A visitor in 1912 found the house 'modern and luxurious', and was impressed by the dinner table 'set with candles in silver candlesticks with red shades, flowers from the conservatory in crystal vases, and six or seven courses of delicious food'. In short, 'one would fancy from the richness of the carpets, beauty of decoration and perfect cuisine, that one had been transported to London, instead of being in the wilds of Skye' (Isobel Macdonald, *A Family in Skye, 1908-1916.*)

DUISDALE HOTEL, ISLE OF SKYE

Isle Ornsay (Ebb-tide Island), c1905. Historically, the village possesses an importance which seems at first glance quite disproportionate to its size. A ruined cell or chapel indicates early religious associations, and an excellent stone jetty was constructed in the eighteenth century for the herring fishing industry. In the nineteenth century, Isle Ornsay featured in MacBrayne's sailing schedules, and in 1897 plans were even mooted to lay a railway line from here to Dunvegan and Uig. This view from the tidal island shows the few residential and commercial buildings grouped around the harbour. Note the small white building with a pyramidal roof on the right. Now a dovecote, this was originally a two-seater toilet with fully automatic flushing, courtesy of the tide. Appropriately, it is situated at a place known locally as Rubha na Faileadh ('The Point of Smells').

Facing the harbour, Isle Ornsay General Stores are flanked by the Post Office (right), and the old meal store and hayloft. The main building is thought to have been built originally in 1812, and at the turn of the century when this picture was taken, eight people worked behind the counter. Operated by the Graham brothers, it was said to have been 'the biggest shop between Skye and Glasgow'. Indeed, on his 1864 visit Alexander Smith commented that 'every conceivable article may be obtained [there]'. Damaged by fire about 1914, the premises (now the offices of Fearann Eilean Iarmain) were gutted again in 1992 with the consequent loss of valuable archival material. The offices have since been rebuilt.

Surrounded by potential customers, Inn-keeper 'Eirtidh Mor' Nicolson, flanked by his two sisters, stands in the doorway of Isle Ornsay Inn on its opening day in 1888. This charred photographic fragment of the occasion was saved from the flames of the devastating fire in 1992. (Photograph reproduced here by kind permission of Sir Iain Noble).

Originally built in 1888, Isle Ornsay Hotel was enlarged by the addition of a glass porch along its frontage in the 1920s. Since acquiring substantial areas of land around Isle Ornsay almost twenty five years ago, Sir Iain Noble has done much to provide employment, together with preserving and promoting the culture of this predominately Gaelic speaking community.

Isle Ornsay Lighthouse.

Top The imposing white tower of this, the third of Skye's lighthouses, is seen here camouflaged against the snow capped mountains of Knoydart. The lighthouse lies at the south-east corner not of Ornsay itself, but on another islet, Eilean Sionnach (Isle of the Fox). Completed in 1857, the engineer Thomas Stevenson cleverly designed a new condensing apparatus, especially suitable for narrow waters, by which the light shown in different directions varied in strength according to the distance from which it was required to be seen. This improvement in the dioptric system was shown at the Great Exhibition of 1851. The light was automated in 1962.

Above A scattering of houses, and a mosaic of croftland around a sheltered bay south of Isle Ornsay make up this 1910 view of Camus Croise. Somewhat unusually this postcard is vertically overprinted, 'R. Graham & Co', and was sold through the Isle Ornsay Stores.

Ord House, 1939. A narrow road crosses the backbone of Sleat and drops down to the shores of Loch Eishort at Ord. Here, there are superb views over Loch Slapin and Strathaird, the Cuillin Ridge and Blaven. This was the setting for Alexander Smith's classic *A Summer in Skye*, published in 1865, and required reading for all those who wish to understand a little of the island. In 1925, the Nicolson family took over Ord House, together with its farm. The Misses Flora and Katie Nicolson opened the house as an hotel in 1947, their brother Kennie ran the farm, and they dispensed old-fashioned Highland hospitality of the very best kind for a period of thirty years.

Another twisting road, with blind summits which demands the full attention of the motorist, brings the traveller from Ord to Tarskavaig township, whose name is said to mean Whale Bay. The scenery is magnificent even for Skye, and the sloping croftlands bear grain crops as heavy as any in the most fertile of the Inner Hebrides. In more recent years, Skye terriers have been bred here, and exported all over the world.

Upper Ostaig House, Skye

Prior to 1870 and its enlargement, Upper Ostaig House was known simply as Ostaig. This building is thought to have replaced an earlier one in which Johnson and Boswell stayed, in late September 1773, as guests of Dr. Martin Macpherson, the then Minister of Sleat. It was 'a pretty good house, built by Macpherson's father, upon a farm near the church'. There was also a library, much to the visitors' liking. Established close by in the 1970s, in the former farm buildings of the Great Steading, Sabal Mor Ostaig now provides a range of higher education, business and cultural studies – in Gaelic, of course.

Surrounded by woods, tall trees and a rookery, Ostaig House house lies between the road to Armadale and the shore. Despite being built in the 1870s, it is sometimes referred to as the 'new house' of Ostaig. Formerly the residence of the late 7th Baronet, Alexander Godfrey Macdonald of Macdonald, it was also home to his son, the present Lord Macdonald, who lived here with his family until 1983.

MACDONALD

CLANSMEN'S CREST : *A hand in armour fessways, holding by its point a cross crosslet fitchy, gules.*

MOTTO : *Per mare per terras (By sea and by land).*

GAELIC NAME : *MacDhomhnuill.*

Top Armadale Castle, 1895. At the beginning of the nineteenth century, Lord Macdonald's estates extended to at least 140,000 acres, and the income he received from his tenants kelp gathering activities alone amounted to £20,000 per annum. In 1815, the architect James Gillespie Graham began to implement His Lordship's plans for the building of this modern seat for the Macdonalds. There had been a house on this site for centuries, and the new building was to be added to the south end of the existing two storey building (far right).

If the exterior was imposing and the setting superb, then the interior would be no less impressive. The fan tracery on the lofty ceilings, the tall mullioned windows and fireplaces made of local Strath marble all combined to give an impression of elegance. Hospitality could be provided on a lavish scale in the new extended castle.

Simultaneous with the building work, a landscaping programme began and the grounds were planted with exotic trees and shrubs. A mound was removed to create the front lawn, and paths, a new walled garden, the main drive and the bridge were built. At the time this photograph was taken, the grounds were maturing and well established, and it would have been impossible to predict that just fifty-two years later the castle would cease to be a family home. (Photograph reproduced here by kind permission of Lord Macdonald).

Above Armadale Castle from the rear, showing the Somerled Window, 1895. The front entrance to the castle was by way of several wide stone steps and a pair of tall ornamental doors, which brought visitors into a lofty entrance hall. In front of them, a staircase led up to a landing, over which was the famous stained glass window. This was a representation of the progenitor of the Clan, the mighty Somerled, *Rex Insularum*, suitably clad in chain mail and menacingly holding a battle-axe. Maximum effect was created when the rays of the afternoon sun filtered through the trees, backlighting the window. A writer in the mid-nineteenth century noted that it was said to have cost five hundred pounds, an enormous sum in those days. Sadly, nothing of it now remains as this part of the castle, which had become dangerous, was dismantled in 1980 to create a sculptured ruin. (Photograph reproduced here by kind permission of Lord Macdonald).

This 1895 picture provides a rare and by no means typical glimpse of life in Skye during the closing years of Queen Victoria's long reign. A pony and trap have been brought up from the Coach House for a children's outing. However, the Great War was less than twenty years away at this time, and would prove to be a watershed. Men from Skye flocked to support the cause upon which Britain had embarked, and the resultant loss of life in the trenches of Northern France and Flanders was immense. Whole communities were devastated, and few were left untouched. After 1914, conditions on the large estates went into decline; land suffered through being unworked, and sporting facilities were unlet, affecting both the proprietors' income and the employment prospects of those who depended on the land for a living. A way of life was vanishing, the Great Depression loomed, and nothing would ever be the same again. (Photograph reproduced here by kind permission of Lord Macdonald).

Visit by the Prince of Wales to Armadale Castle, 1895. Queen Victoria's love affair with the Highlands probably started about 1847, the year Her Majesty and Prince Albert made a voyage up the West Coast between the Clyde and Fort William. They had given the royal seal of approval to cruising in West Highland waters, and the itinerary they had taken was known thereafter as 'The Royal Route'. In the following year the Queen first set eyes upon Balmoral, and it was purchased four years later in 1852. Here, seated on the castle steps at Armadale, the Prince of Wales (later King Edward VII), binoculars in hand, joins this family group for a photograph commemorating his visit. (Photograph reproduced here by kind permission of Lord Macdonald).

Armadale Castle, coach house and stable block restoration. When it became clear that impending death duties would result in the entire loss of the remaining Macdonald Estates, the Clan Donald Lands Trust was formed, in 1972, after an appeal to Clansmen. Their generosity enabled 14,300 acres of land to be purchased around the castle, thus saving this foothold in Sleat and placing it under permanent protection. Vast improvements have since been made to the grounds, with dangerous parts of the castle being made safe, and museum and exhibition facilities provided in the oldest part of the castle. In this 1984 photograph, the stable block (built around 1820 for £2000), is in the final stages of the restoration and conversion project which cost £1m. Now the hub of the Clan Donald Centre, it has won a variety of awards and is a major tourist attraction providing two luxurious flats on the first floor, and a shop, restaurant and administrative facilities below.

The first public jetty was built at Armadale in 1872, but it was not a deep water pier, and calling steamers were consequently forced to lie off-shore and await a rendezvous with a rowing boat in order to discharge passengers. The mails and supplies were also collected and brought back to be landed on the exposed rocks at low water or, if tides permitted, picked up by horse and cart from the bay itself. These ladies, gazing out to sea in 1895, could not have imagined that the first of Armadale's deep water piers would be built over these rocks nineteen years later, in 1914. (Photograph reproduced here by kind permission of Lord Macdonald).

Armadale Pier. Skye.

The newly constructed wooden pier, photographed here in 1915, was intended as a
'temporary' facility, although it was to be thirty years before a more permanent structure
was put in place. Even this was subsequently expanded (in May 1994) when Armadale pier
was adapted to provide roll-on/roll-off facilities. A far cry indeed from the simple wooden
structure of eighty years previously.

THE PIER, ARMADALE, SKYE.   222103. JV.

Several conveyances await passengers coming ashore at Armadale Pier in this 1935 picture.
There was intense rivalry between two local taxi owners who, it was said, were not above
playing a variety of tricks on each other in order to gain custom. But some thought that a
herring tied to a hot exhaust was going too far!

A handful of passengers from the SS *Claymore* step ashore at Armadale in this 1930s photograph. Following the introduction of roll-on/roll-off facilities recently, it is interesting to note the latest figures for the Mallaig to Armadale service. During 1994, 36,312 cars, 153,636 passengers and 771 coaches were conveyed over this route. On Skye, the traffic joins the main A851 road to Broadford, originally constructed in 1812. Even today, following the upgraded facilities at the pier, this is still a single track road.

Armadale and Ardvasar are contiguous. The former has a Celtic name, the latter is Norse, and this aptly illustrates how quite different characteristics intermingle and coexist alongside each other throughout the island. The village General Stores and Post Office are situated on the extreme right of the group of buildings pictured. Ardvasar became the terminus of the rural post from Broadford in 1863; previously, semi-private postal arrangements operated only as far as Armadale Castle, where the foot runners left their bags.

Ardvasar Village, seen here under a mantle of snow at the turn of the century. At 57°N, this part of Skye is on the same latitude as Labrador, but the west coast of Scotland has the advantage of the moderating influence of the warm waters brought by the Atlantic Gulf Stream, resulting in milder, more humid weather. As a result, snow at low levels does not tend to last long in Sleat. However, Skye experienced particularly severe blizzards in 1881, and again in January 1945, when drifts twenty feet deep required some townships to be supplied by sea.

On the day in 1864 that Alexander Smith described the Ardvasar Hotel as 'a plain inn [standing] by the wayside where refreshments may be procured', he came to know Ardvasar quite well. At that time, the village consisted of some twenty houses. While he was anxiously waiting for a sighting of the steamer (which was unusually late), he marked time by walking around the locality and looking out of the inn, where he also had tea. Somewhat wearily he recorded: 'It is difficult to kill time anywhere, but at this little Skye clachan, it is more difficult than anywhere else'. The hotel was built as a coaching inn early in the eighteenth century, and as such is one of the older establishments on the west coast of Scotland. During most of its existence it was part of the formerly extensive Macdonald Estates. One of only two licensed premises in Sleat (the other being at Isle Ornsay) when this photograph was taken in the thirties, the hotel played an essential part in the life of the community, as it does now in this, the most southerly part of Skye.

POST OFFICE, ARDVASAR, SKYE.

The Ardvasar Post Office building, pictured here in the 1930s, can be spied at a bend in the road in the previous photograph showing the hotel, and it remained on this site for a little over fifty years. We can assume it is a very warm day on this occasion, as the post office door is fully open, as are the front and side windows. On the left, a little haymaking is under way.

The four miles of twisting road from Ardvasar to the Point of Sleat, the local Land's End, terminates at Aird. About halfway along its length at a sharp bend lies the entrance to Tormore House, which can be seen below the road, near the shore among trees and gardens. James and Donald Macdonald, the former of whom was the Sleat factor, were tenants in 1773 at the time of Johnson and Boswell's visit. When this photograph was taken in 1905, Tormore, a part of the Macdonald Estates in Sleat, was regularly let to shooting tenants.

EPILOGUE

The way it was, 1905

The Skye bridge under construction, from Kyleakin, April 1995.